easy
italian
in minutes

This edition first published in Great Britain in 2006 by
Kyle Cathie Limited

ISBN 978 1 85626 628 4

10 9 8 7 6 5 4 3

Senior editor: Helen Woodhall
Designer: Geoff Hayes
Stylist: Penny Markham
Home economist: Annie Nichols
Production: Sha Huxtable and Alice Holloway

Colour reproduction by Scanhouse Pty Ltd
Printed and bound in China by C & C Offset Printers

With special thanks to: Linda Bain, Nicola Donovan, Amanda
Fries, Sarah Lee, Kate McBain

With thanks and acknowledgment to all the recipe writers whose
talents have contributed to the creation of this book.

First published in Great Britain in 2005 by Kyle Cathie Ltd for
Sainsbury's Supermarkets Ltd

Kyle Cathie Limited
122 Arlington Road
London NW1 7HP
www.kylecathie.com

**The eggs used in this book are medium sized. All spoon
measurements for dry ingredients are heaped. 1 teaspoon =
5ml, 1 tablespoon = 15ml. Always use either metric or
imperial measurements when following a recipe – never mix
the two.**

contents

introduction

Succulent Parma ham; irresistibly fresh tomato and basil soup; risotto and pasta dishes topped with lavish shavings of Parmesan cheese; pizza, pesto and pannetone; wickedly indulgent tiramisù – the British have adopted Italian food so thoroughly that we may even have forgotten that it was ever exotic. The reasons for the appeal of Italian food are obvious. It's healthy and wholesome, robust, down-to-earth and simply delicious.

Antipasto

Italian cuisine is based on the finest ingredients simply cooked or, in the case of many snacks and salads, not cooked at all. Italian cookery uses a huge range of preserved, smoked and dried meat products which vary from region to region. Authentic Parma ham can only be made in Parma and is stamped with a crown symbol representing the ancient duchy of that city. Bresaola, the beef

equivalent, is made by rubbing a lean leg of beef with salt and spices and leaving it to air-dry for several months. The result is a luscious lean, dark red meat with a smoky tang to it. And then there is salami, a garlic sausage made everywhere from the deep south to Piedmont, and subtly different in each place.

These meats are all best served at or just above room temperature with various salad accompaniments. Try Parma Ham with Fresh Figs (page 17), Bresaola and Rocket Salad with Parmesan (page 18) or Warm Salami, Rosemary and Potato Salad (page 20). A starter that will carry you straight off to the Tuscan sunshine is Bruschetta (page 23) – rustic bread grilled and served warm, smeared with garlic and olive oil and topped with white beans and rosemary, anchovy and lemon zest, Mediterranean vegetables or whatever is seasonal and tickles your fancy. Our version contrasts the glorious reds of tomatoes and peppers with the darker tones of black olives.

Pasta

No Italian meal is complete without pasta. Fresh pasta is extremely simple to make and very tasty. If you don't have a pasta-making machine, you can still experiment with different shapes – try our suggestions on page 120. Some of the popular pasta shapes used in this book are:

Tagliatelle: long, flat ribbon-like strips, traditionally served with a rich creamy sauce

8

hat will just coat the pasta. Pappardelle is similar, but with broader strips.

Fusilli: shorter, corkscrew-shaped twirls, best served with a sauce that has small morsels of chopped vegetables, meat or herbs which will be trapped in the twists. Fusilli often comes as *tricolore* – three-coloured – with tomato paste added to make the pasta orange and spinach to make it green. Try this with lemon and fennel (page 36) – scrumptious!

Penne: short, quill-shaped pasta that can be boiled and served with a sauce like most pastas, or added to a casserole-style dish to be baked in the oven.

Ravioli: normally made into small parcels stuffed with meat and baked with a tomato sauce, but can also be served as flat rectangles of pasta as in Open Ravioli with Asparagus and Sage Butter (page 44).

Whatever shape you decide on and whatever sauce you choose, the sauce should be just enough to coat the pasta, not overwhelm it.

Rice
Risotto is another mouthwatering Italian classic. It has thousands of variations, but they all agree on one thing – the best risotto is made with arborio rice, fried briefly in a light coating of olive oil, then boiled in stock (and sometimes wine) to make it tasty and succulent. Our Milanese Risotto (page 32) is based on the traditional approach, but we've also included a Quick Walnut and Mushroom Risotto (page 50) that will come in handy when you have rice left over!

Pizza
The traditional Italian pizza base is thin and crispy (you can make your own following the recipe on page 116); in its simplest form it is topped with nothing more than mozzarella cheese (another speciality of the Neapolitan region) tomatoes, basil and olive oil. This is the classic margherita pizza, named after one of the queens of Savoy. We have given just this recipe (page 48) because once you have mastered the basics, the choice of toppings is limited only by your imagination and the fresh ingredients available. Mushrooms, sweet peppers, capers, anchovies, clams, ham or dried meats, eggs and spinach – in any combination that takes your fancy – are just some of the ingredients you may choose to spread over your tomato and mozzarella.

Vegetables and herbs
Italian cuisine is nothing if not colourful, and nowhere is this more obvious than in the delicious fresh vegetables and herbs grown all over the country. We've talked about tomatoes – there are so many varieties, eaten every day fresh, canned or in sauces that we could have filled a whole book with them – but that would have meant overlooking the aubergines,

asparagus and artichokes, fennel and fagioli beans, onions, peppers and garlic... The hearty Tuscan Bean and Vegetable Soup (page 31) is a warming reminder that even in this sun-drenched country there are wintry days when comfort food is welcome. Further north, tender fresh asparagus is served as an appetiser with the local creamy butter. And then there are the sweet peppers, fried in lashings of olive oil to make Peperonata (page 79), pure brilliant colour on a plate.

Rich colours abound in the salad vegetables, too. Plenty of bright, fresh greens, of course, but also the black-leafed cabbage cavolo nero (see Pappardelle with Pancetta and Cavolo Nero, page 38) and reddish-purple radicchio, eaten raw in salads to give a sharp, zingy taste, or cooked like spinach and baked in the oven as in our Baked Penne with Dolcelatte and Radicchio (page 43).

Basil is the quintessential Italian herb, used by itself as a flavouring and garnish, or as the main ingredient of pesto (page 114), an indispensable accompaniment to pasta, soups and other dishes. Sage, rosemary, thyme, parsley and fennel also add zest to dishes such as Chicken Livers on Chargrilled Polenta (page 56), Garlic and Rosemary Lamb (page 64) and Tuscan Potato Salad (page 92).

Oil and vinegar
Olive oil and balsamic vinegar – our mouths start to water at the very mention of the

names. More than anything else they put Italian food in a class of its own. Tuscan olive oil is legendary and the area produces flavours for every taste, from soft and fruity to more nutty oils. There's hardly a savoury dish in this book that doesn't contain olive o but Parmesan-crusted Fish with Tomato and Olive Dressing (page 52) and Fruity Baked Aubergines and Peppers (page 86) are two that show it at its best.

The word vinegar doesn't really do justice to the luxurious, rich and fragrant sweet-sour liquid called balsamic vinegar. Just a drop or two added to sauces and dressings, or drizzled over fish, meat, vegetables and even fruit is enough to let its flavour out. True balsamic vinegar can only be made in the Modena area of Emilia Romagna. Taste the difference when you fry tomatoes in it in Pan Fried Steak with Herby Polenta (page 68).

Cheese
Cheese features at almost every stage of the Italian meal, from the irresistible Parmesan Crisps (page 14) to Griddled Sirloin Steak wit Gorgonzola (page 71).

Parmesan is grated or shaved over almost everything, while mozzarella is essential to pizza and to salads where it is combined wit tomato and basil (page 74). The best mozzarella is made from buffalo milk but yo increasingly find it made from cow's milk too Creamy, tangy, blue-veined and almost swee

า flavour, Gorgonzola is a superb dessert heese, but also good in sauces for risotto nd pasta, and in stuffings. If the taste is too trong for you, use dolcelatte – a gentle blue heese whose name means 'sweet milk'. Mascarpone, a creamy cheese with a taste nd texture similar to those of crème fraîche, s a must in rich, luscious desserts such as ฿ruléed Fruit with Amaretto & Mascarpone page 98).

HOW TO USE THIS BOOK: We've divided the recipes according to the courses of a meal, with a separate chapter on vegetables and another on basics such as pasta dough and pizza bases. We have given preparation and cooking times to help with planning and, as a guide, there are also calorie and fat counts for each dish.

starters

parmesan crisps

The perfect accompaniment to a glass of wine before dinner, or as a soup garnish.

30 mins		57 cals	4g fat
prep & cook time	makes approx. 24	per serving	per serving

50g (2oz) Parmesan, grated
1 sheet baking parchment

Preheat the grill until hot.

Cover the grill tray with baking parchment. Place little rounds of grated Parmesan (about the size of a twopence piece) over the parchment, spacing them out well to allow for spreading. There will be approximately 24 crisps.

Grill until golden and slightly brown.

Leave to cool on the parchment and peel off gently. Eat straightaway or store in an airtight container until needed.

COOK'S TIPS
When buying Parmesan, choose Parmigiano Reggiano, the official version of this classic hard cheese, the strong and fragrant flavour of which makes it a staple of Italian cookery.

The crisps can be moulded into different shapes before they cool. Roll around the handle of a wooden spoon, or oil the base of a small jar and mould a warm crisp around the end to make small 'baskets'.

Be careful not to overcook, or they will become bitter tasting.

parma ham with fresh figs

Succulent figs and salty ham combine to make a simple starter that takes just minutes to prepare.

15 mins		242 cals	8g fat
prep time	serves 4-6	per serving	per serving

12 ripe green or black figs
12 slices of paper-thin Parma ham
fresh ciabatta or focaccia bread
unsalted butter

Wipe the figs with a damp cloth and dry them with kitchen paper. Using a sharp knife, cut the figs into halves.

Arrange the slices of ham and the figs alternately on a platter and serve with bread and butter.

Variation
Replace the figs with deseeded portions of sweet ripe melon. Grind over a few twists of black pepper to serve.

Parma ham is also known as *prosciutto crudo* - literally 'raw ham' - referring to the fact that it is cured rather than cooked.

bresaola & rocket salad with parmesan

Another simple starter combining the flavour and texture of three classic Italian ingredients.

15 mins	serves 6	99 cals	7g fat
prep time	serves 6	per serving	per serving

50g (2oz) rocket leaves
75g (3oz) Bresaola
25g (1oz) Parmesan, shaved
1 tablespoon virgin olive oil
1 lemon, quartered
salt and freshly ground black pepper

Arrange the rocket leaves on a serving plate and arrange the slices of Bresaola on top. Sprinkle over the Parmesan shavings and serve drizzled with the olive oil. Squeeze the lemon juice on top and season to taste.

COOK'S TIP
To make Parmesan shavings, simply draw a potato peeler down the longest edge of the cheese to make long narrow strips.

Bresaola is made by rubbing a lean leg of beef with salt and spices and leaving it to air-dry for several months. This results in a lean dark red meat with a smoky tang to it.

warm salami, rosemary & potato salad

Strong flavours combine in this gutsy salad to create a starter that will really shake up your taste buds.

prep & cook time — serves 4 — 392 cals per serving — 27g fat per serving

2 teaspoons olive oil
175g (6oz) sliced salami, quartered
2-3 salad onions or 1/2 small red onion, finely chopped
small clove garlic, crushed
250g (8oz) new potatoes, eg Charlotte or Anya, cooked
50g (2oz) pitted black olives, quartered
125g (4oz) artichoke antipasto, drained
1-2 teaspoons freshly chopped rosemary
salt and freshly ground black pepper
150g (5oz) bistro salad leaves or mixed herb salad

COOK'S TIP
Double the quantity of potatoes and serve as a main course for lunch or light supper.

Charlotte, Anya, Belle de Fontenay and Pink Fir Apple are all good varieties of potato to use in salads.

Heat the oil in a frying pan, add the salami and cook for 3-4 minutes until crispy and golden.

Stir in the onion and garlic and cook for 1 minute.

Stir in the potatoes, cutting the larger ones in half first, the olives, artichokes, rosemary and plenty of seasoning to taste.

Remove from the heat and toss in the salad leaves. Serve immediately.

Variation
Replace the salami with pancetta cubetti, small chunks of sweet, Italian-style bacon.

rustic bruschetta

A real Italian favourite, bruschetta makes a great starter
or light lunch.

prep & cook time	serves 10-12	per serving	per serving

1 ciabatta loaf, sliced into 1cm (1/2in) slices
3 tablespoons olive oil
2 large red peppers
1 small red onion, finely chopped
2 cloves garlic, crushed
8 plum tomatoes, chopped
50g (2oz) black olives
1 tablespoon dried basil
salt and freshly ground black pepper

Preheat the oven to 200°C/400°F/gas mark 6.

Place the ciabatta slices on baking trays, sprinkle
with 2 tablespoons of the oil, and bake for 5
minutes until golden.

Sprinkle the remaining oil over the peppers, place
in a roasting tin and bake for 15 minutes. While
the peppers are still hot, place them in a plastic
bag or a large bowl covered with clingfilm and
leave to steam until cooled, then peel off the skin,
deseed and roughly chop the flesh.

Place the peppers in a bowl with the remaining
ingredients and mix well.

Heap the salsa on top of the toasted bread and
serve immediately.

Variations

Mix chopped ripe vine tomatoes with
anchovies, heap the mixture onto bruschetta,
drizzle with olive oil and sprinkle with
fresh herbs.

For real garlic lovers, rub the ciabatta slices
with a cut clove of garlic before adding the
topping.

COOK'S TIP
**Try making your own ciabatta using the
recipe on page 118.**

cheese, parma ham & honey crostini

Honey, ham, melting cheese and crunchy bread add up to an irresistible combination of flavours and textures.

prep & cook time	serves 6-8	per serving	per serving
30 mins		274 cals	11g fat

1 clove garlic, finely chopped
2 tablespoons olive oil
4 tablespoons runny honey
half baguette cut into 8 slices and toasted
150g (5oz) ball of mozzarella, cut into
   8 slices
100g (3¹/₂oz) Parma ham
8 fresh basil leaves

Mix together the garlic, oil and 2 tablespoons of the honey and spread it over the sliced baguette.

Lay a slice of mozzarella on each slice of toast and place under a hot grill until the cheese melts.

Scrunch a piece of Parma ham on top of each crostini, top with the fresh basil leaves and drizzle with the remaining honey, then serve immediately.

Variation
Use smoked mozzarella for an extra dimension of flavour.

Try other toppings:

Red Pesto and Pepper Crostini Spread a little red pesto onto each crostini, and top with a few roasted red peppers.

Brie and Grape Crostini Top each slice of toast with a slice of Brie and 2 grapes.

Olive and Almond Crostini Purée 100g (3¹/₂oz) olives, 2 tablespoons capers, 4 tablespoons olive oil, a clove of garlic and 50g (2oz) ground almonds in the food processor until combined and use to top the crostini.

gorgonzola & pine kernel pâté

The sharp flavour of this traditional Italian cheese gives this pâté real bite.

30 mins
prep & cook time

serves 6

220 cals
per serving

19g fat
per serving

2 eggs, hard boiled
250g (8oz) Gorgonzola, crumbled
50g (2oz) butter
2 tablespoons pine kernels, toasted lightly in
   a dry frying pan
melted butter (optional)

Separate the cooked egg yolks from the whites. Blend the cheese with the egg yolks and butter.

Chop the egg whites finely and stir them and the pine kernels into the mixture. Transfer to a small dish and chill thoroughly. Serve on its own or with toast.

This potted cheese will keep for 2-3 days in the refrigerator; if you need to keep it a little longer (up to 10 days), cover with a thin layer of melted butter.

fresh tomato & basil soup

Two more classic Italian ingredients combine in this simple starter or tasty light lunch.

prep & cook time	serves 6	per serving	per serving

1 tablespoon olive oil
1 large onion, diced
750g (1½lb) ripe tomatoes
150ml (¼ pint) vegetable stock
1 litre (1¾ pint) tomato juice
20g (¾oz) fresh basil leaves, shredded
2 tablespoons single cream (optional)
salt and freshly ground black pepper

Heat the oil in a saucepan, add the onion and cook for 8-10 minutes until softened and lightly golden.

Take half the tomatoes and halve them. Add to the pan with the onion and cook for a further 5 minutes, breaking down with a spoon.

Pierce the remaining tomatoes and place in a bowl of boiling water for 20 seconds to remove the skins. Cut into chunks, removing the seeds, and set to one side.

Place the onion mixture in a blender with the stock and blend until smooth. Pass through a sieve to remove the skin and pips and return to the pan with the tomato juice, seasoning, half the basil leaves and the diced tomatoes.

Heat through and serve sprinkled with the remaining basil and swirled with cream if desired. Delicious served with warm bread.

COOK'S TIPS
Use tomatoes on the vine for extra flavour - the riper the better.

Dried basil may be substituted for the fresh herb, but remember to use it sparingly as the flavour is more concentrated.

uscan bean & vegetable soup

ou can whip up this hearty rustic soup in no time at all.

30 mins
rep & ok time

serves 4

309 cals
per serving

19g fat
per serving

medium onion
clove garlic
stick celery
large carrot
5g (1oz) butter
tablespoon olive oil
x 425g (14oz) tin mixed bean salad, drained
x 400g (13oz) tin chopped tomatoes
00ml (1½ pints) vegetable stock
teaspoon dried oregano
tablespoons pesto sauce, plus extra to
garnish
medium courgettes
tablespoons soured cream
alt and freshly ground black pepper

eel and finely chop the onion and garlic. Trim
nd chop the celery, and peel and finely chop the
arrot. Melt the butter with the oil in a large
aucepan and gently fry the vegetables for 5
inutes until just tender.

tir in the beans, tomatoes and stock. Add the
regano, pesto and season to taste. Bring to the
oil and simmer for 10 minutes. Trim and dice
he courgettes and add to the soup. Cook for a
urther 5 minutes until all the vegetables are
nder.

Ladle the soup into warmed bowls and top with
the soured cream and pesto sauce. Serve with
crusty bread.

Variations
This recipe can be used as the basis for many
variations. Use any vegetable in season instead
of or as well as courgette: try adding cubes of
pumpkin, or shredded cabbage or spinach.
Remember to add them in order of cooking time
– pumpkin or sweet potato will need to be added
at the same time as the beans, while spinach
should go in at the last minute. To make a more
substantial soup, add small pasta shapes at the
same time as the beans.

See page 114 for home-made pesto.

milanese risotto

Served before a light main meal, this luxurious risotto is a real treat

prep & cook time	serves 2-3	per serving	per serving
30 mins		568 cals	34g fat

2 tablespoons olive oil

175g (6oz) arborio rice

450ml (¾ pint) fresh vegetable stock

150ml (¼ pint) dry white Italian wine

1 pinch saffron strands, soaked in 1 tablespoon
  hot water

75g (3oz) freshly grated Parmesan

50ml (2fl oz) double cream

25g (1oz) Parmesan shavings, to garnish

salt and freshly ground black pepper

Heat the oil in a large pan over a moderate heat.
Add the rice, stir well to coat each grain with oil,
and heat gently for 1 minute. Place the stock and
wine in another pan and bring to the boil.

Add the boiling stock and wine to the rice little
by little, stirring all the while, and adding more
liquid as it is absorbed. After 5 minutes add the
soaked saffron strands, then continue to add the
stock gradually. This will take about 15-20
minutes.

The risotto is cooked when the rice is al dente
(cooked through but with a slight bite in the
centre of each grain). It should not be too dry –
it should be sloppy enough to spread out on the
plate when you serve it rather than staying in
one lump. Add the grated Parmesan and cream,
stir well to incorporate, and season to taste.

Ladle into individual bowls, scatter over the
Parmesan shavings and serve immediately.

COOK'S TIP

For a perfect result, you need to stir the
risotto continuously. This action breaks down
the starch in the rice grains, which makes for
a perfectly creamy, sauce-like consistency.

Don't try to make this risotto with ordinary
long-grain or Basmati rice. Its success
depends on the high starch content of risotto
rices such as arborio, carnaroli or vialone
nero.

Variation

Use half-fat crème fraîche in place of the cream
for a lower fat alternative.

main courses

fusilli tricolore with lemon & fennel

The sharp citrus tang of lemon cuts through the sweet aniseed flavour of fennel to get your taste buds really tingling.

30 mins		326 cals	10g fat
prep & cook time	serves 2	per serving	per serving

250g (8oz) fusilli tricolore
1 bulb fennel, roughly chopped
2 cloves garlic, chopped
2 tablespoons olive oil
150ml (¼ pint) white wine
zest and juice of 1 lemon
20g (³/₄oz) flat-leaf parsley, chopped
Parmesan, freshly grated, to serve
salt and freshly ground black pepper

Cook the pasta in a large pan of boiling water following the instructions on the pack.

Meanwhile, place the fennel, garlic and olive oil in a saucepan and cook with the lid on over a moderate heat for 10-15 minutes until soft. Add the wine, lemon juice and seasoning and cook for a further 1-2 minutes. Add the zest of the lemon.

Drain the pasta, reserving a little of the water to combine with the sauce. Add the sauce to the pasta and finish with the parsley.

Serve immediately with freshly grated Parmesan.

COOK'S TIP
As a rough guide, use approximately 65g (2¹/₂oz) of dried pasta per person for a starter, and 125g (4oz) for a main course.

pappardelle with pancetta & cavolo nero

Cavolo nero is a curly black cabbage that dates back to Roman times. Crinkly green cabbage works just as well.

30 mins		671 cals	38g fat
prep & cook time	serves 2	per serving	per serving

125g (4oz) pappardelle
1 tablespoon olive oil
125g (4oz) pancetta cubetti
2 cloves garlic, finely chopped
100g (3½oz) cavolo nero, stalks removed and roughly chopped
75ml (3fl oz) white wine
2 tablespoons double cream, crème fraîche or half-fat
 crème fraîche
2 tablespoons freshly grated Parmesan
salt and freshly ground black pepper

Heat a large saucepan of salted water and bring to the boil. Add the pasta and cook for 6-8 minutes, until al dente (still retains a 'bite').

Meanwhile, heat the oil in a medium saucepan and when hot add the pancetta and garlic. Cook for 2-3 minutes until the pancetta is slightly crisp.

Add the cavolo nero and stir to wilt in the oil. Season with salt and freshly ground black pepper. Add the wine and boil for 2-3 minutes until reduced. Add the cream and Parmesan and heat through. Drain the pasta, stir into the sauce and serve immediately.

Pancetta cubetti are small chunks of sweet, Italian-style bacon. Alternatively, use cubes of thick-cut streaky bacon.

conchiglie with griddled chicken, basil & rocket

This summery pasta dish is colourful as well as delicious.

30 mins		701 cals	38g fat
prep & cook time	serves 4	per serving	per serving

250g (8oz) conchiglie pasta
4 tablespoons olive oil
1 bundle asparagus, trimmed
4 chicken breasts, skinless
125g (4oz) rocket
8 sun-dried tomatoes, cut into fine strips
25g (1oz) pine kernels, lightly toasted in a dry frying pan
25g (1oz) Parmesan, finely grated
20g (³/₄oz) purple or green fresh basil
salt and freshly ground black pepper

Cook the pasta in plenty of boiling salted water for 10 minutes. Whilst you are doing this heat a griddle pan or heavy frying pan, brush the asparagus with a small amount of oil and cook over a medium heat for about 3 minutes on each side. Remove from the pan and keep warm. In the same pan cook the chicken for about 5 minutes on each side or until cooked (the juices should run clear when a skewer is inserted into the centre of the breast).

When the pasta is cooked, drain well. Heat the remaining oil in a large saucepan and quickly cook the rocket until wilted, then add the pasta, asparagus, tomatoes, pine kernels, Parmesan, basil and seasoning, and mix well to combine.

Divide the pasta between 4 plates and top with a chicken breast. Serve.

Replace the chicken breast with cubes of mozzarella for a vegetarian alternative.

baked penne with dolcelatte & radicchio

real comfort food that can be prepared in advance and popped in the oven just before you're ready to eat.

30 mins		713 cals	61g fat
prep & cook time	serves 4	per serving	per serving

250g (8oz) penne rigate
50g (2oz) butter
250g (8oz) button mushrooms, sliced
2 cloves garlic, chopped finely
1 tablespoon finely chopped fresh sage
1 small head of radicchio (250-275g/8-9oz), cored and shredded finely
250ml (8fl oz) double cream, or half-fat crème fraîche
50g (2oz) Parmesan, finely grated
175g (6oz) dolcelatte, cubed
fresh sage leaves, to garnish
salt and freshly ground black pepper

Preheat the oven to 230°C/450°F/gas mark 8.

Butter a 23 x 28cm (9 x 11in) ovenproof dish.

Cook the pasta in a large pan of boiling water, following the pack instruction, until al dente.

Meanwhile, melt the butter in a large frying pan and fry the mushrooms and garlic for about 5 minutes until softened. Stir in the sage and radicchio and remove the pan from the heat.

In a large bowl stir together the cream, Parmesan and dolcelatte. Add the mushroom mixture and pasta. Taste and season.

Transfer the mixture to the ovenproof dish and bake in the oven for 12-15 minutes, or until the top is browned and bubbly.

Serve garnished with fresh sage leaves.

Radicchio is a variety of leaf vegetable with reddish-purple leaves. It can be eaten raw in salads, or cooked, like spinach or cabbage, as a vegetable.

Dolcelatte is a mild, creamy, blue-veined cheese with a slightly crumbly texture whose name literally means 'sweet milk'. Goat's cheese can be used in this dish instead of dolcelatte.

open ravioli with asparagus & sage butter

A modern twist on an old favourite - large open ravioli are easy to make and look great on the plate.

prep & cook time	serves 4	per serving	per serving
30 mins		629 cals	35g fat

300g (10oz) asparagus
250ml (8fl oz) white wine
125g (4oz) butter, cut into tiny cubes
1 teaspoon white wine vinegar
10g ($^1/_3$oz) fresh sage, finely chopped
250g (8oz) fresh lasagne sheets
125g (4oz) Parma ham, cut into strips
40g (1$^1/_2$oz) Parmesan, shaved
salt and freshly ground black pepper

Cook the asparagus gently with the tips out of the water for 3-4 minutes until tender to the point of a knife.

Heat the wine and reduce the liquid to 1 teaspoon then slowly add the butter over a low heat. Add the vinegar and season to taste. Carefully fold in the chopped sage.

Cook the fresh lasagne sheets according to the pack instructions.

Arrange one lasagne sheet on a plate and spread with a little sage butter, then place some of the cooked asparagus and strips of Parma ham on top. Layer up with further sheets of lasagne and filling. Repeat for the 3 other portions, top with Parmesan shavings, and serve.

It's not complicated to make your own lasagne sheets for this recipe - just follow the recipe on page 120.

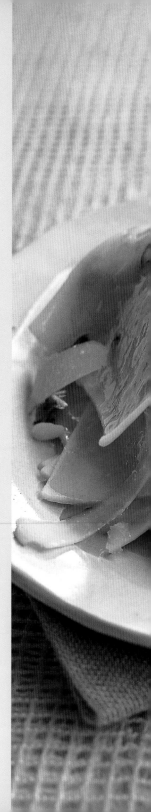

sweet potato gnocchi with rocket pesto

Sweet potato gives this Italian classic a deliciously smoky flavour.

30 mins	serves 4	624 cals	37g fat
prep & cook time	serves 4	per serving	per serving

625g (1¼lb) sweet potato, peeled and diced
15g (½oz) butter
75g (3oz) plain flour
100g (3½oz) semolina
freshly grated nutmeg
salt and freshly ground black pepper

Rocket pesto:
50g (2oz) rocket
2 garlic cloves, crushed
3 tablespoons pine kernels
100ml (3½fl oz) olive oil

Cook the sweet potatoes in boiling salted water for 10 minutes or until just tender. Drain and leave to cool.

Place all the ingredients for the pesto in a food processor or pound with a pestle and mortar to make a coarse paste.

Mash the potatoes in a large bowl until smooth. Add the butter, flour, semolina, nutmeg, salt and pepper. Mix to a dough. Divide the dough into four pieces and shape each piece into a long roll about 2cm (¾in) thick. Cut each roll across into equal-size rounds. Bring a large saucepan of salted water to the boil. Drop the gnocchi into the water in batches and cook for 3–5 minutes until they rise to the surface. Remove with a slotted spoon. Once all the gnocchi are cooked, stir in the pesto and serve.

Variation
To make classic gnocchi, see page 122. Use home-made pesto Genovese (page 114) instead of rocket pesto.

cheat's margherita pizza

An old favourite on the table in minutes.

25 mins		**402** cals	**9**g fat
prep & cook time	serves 2	per serving	per serving

4 tablespoons tomato pizza topping
1 thin and crispy pizza base
50g (2oz) mozzarella, grated
1 plum tomato, sliced
4 basil leaves, torn
pinch oregano

Preheat the oven to 220ºC/425ºF/gas mark 7.

Spread the topping over the pizza base. Sprinkle the mozzarella evenly over the base. Arrange the sliced tomatoes on top and sprinkle over the basil leaves and oregano.

Bake for 10-12 minutes or until golden and crisp.

COOK'S TIP
To make your own pizza base and tomato sauce, see the recipes on page 116 and page 112.

Variations
Your imagination is the only limit! Try these Italian classics for starters:
Marinara - tomato, anchovy, garlic and black olives
Frutti di Mare (seafood) - tomato and garlic sprinkled with a couple of handfuls of mixed seafood such as prawns, mussels and squid rings.
Quattro Formaggi (four cheeses) - tomato and four Italian cheeses such as mozzarella, Gorgonzola, bel paese, taleggio, Parmesan.
Vegetariana - tomato, mozzarella, mixed roast vegetables, garlic and black olives.

quick walnut & mushroom risotto

A great way of using up leftover rice, this is an easy variation on the classic risotto (see page 32).

30 mins	serves 4	390 cals	23g fat
prep & cook time	serves 4	per serving	per serving

2 tablespoons olive oil or 25g (1oz) butter
1 onion, finely chopped
250g (8oz) large flat mushrooms, chopped
75g (3oz) walnuts, roughly chopped
6 cloves
1/4 teaspoon grated nutmeg
100ml (3 1/2 fl oz) white wine
400g (13oz) cooked long-grain rice
1 tablespoon double cream
chopped fresh parsley, to garnish
salt and freshly ground black pepper

Heat the olive oil or butter in a large saucepan, add the onion and fry gently for 5-10 minutes until it begins to brown.

Add the mushrooms, walnuts and spices and cook for 5 minutes, or until the mushrooms have begun to soften, adding a little more oil or butter, if necessary. Add the wine, season and simmer for a further 2 minutes until the mushrooms are tender.

Stir in the rice and cream and heat through gently, stirring constantly. Remove the cloves, if you can find them, and serve hot, garnished with chopped parsley.

Variation
The sauce is also delicious served with freshly cooked pasta.

parmesan-crusted haddock with tomato & olive dressing

Crunchy-topped fish is complemented by a flavour-packed dressing for a light and delicious main course.

30 mins		**347** cals	**16g** fat
prep & cook time	serves 4	per serving	per serving

75g (3oz) fresh white breadcrumbs
50g (2oz) Parmesan, freshly grated
20g (³⁄₄oz) flat-leaf parsley, chopped
4 haddock fillets, or other firm-fleshed fish, such as cod
1 tablespoon olive oil
salt and freshly ground black pepper

For the dressing:
4 plum tomatoes, skin and seeds removed, chopped
50g (2oz) Kalamata olives, pitted and chopped
2 tablespoons olive oil
20g (³⁄₄oz) basil leaves, torn
salt and freshly ground black pepper

Preheat the oven to 190°C/375°F/gas mark 5.

Mix together the breadcrumbs, Parmesan and parsley, and season to taste.

Brush the haddock fillets with the olive oil and coat with the breadcrumb mixture. Place on a baking sheet in the preheated oven and cook for 15 minutes or until cooked through and golden brown.

Mix together the dressing ingredients, season to taste, and serve with the fish.

florentine crab cakes with tarragon & mustard mayonnaise

Spinach gives a new twist to an old family favourite.
Skip the mayo for a lower-fat alternative.

30 mins
prep & cook time

serves 4

836 cals
per serving

69g fat
per serving

40g (1½oz) unsalted butter
75g (3oz) shallots, peeled and finely chopped
2 cloves garlic, peeled and finely chopped
500g (1lb) fresh spinach, washed and stalks
    removed
2 x 175g (6oz) tins crabmeat in brine
75g (3oz) fresh white breadcrumbs
175g (6oz) ball mozzarella, grated
1 egg yolk
2 tablespoons oil for frying
200ml (7fl oz) mayonnaise
1 tablespoon English mustard
2 tablespoons wholegrain mustard
10g (⅓oz) fresh tarragon, finely chopped
freshly ground black pepper

Preheat the oven to 200°C/400°F/gas mark 6.

Melt the butter over a medium heat and gently fry the shallots for 2–3 minutes without colouring. Add the garlic and fry for a further minute. Add the spinach slowly, stirring frequently. When the spinach has wilted and cooked, but is still bright green, remove from the heat and drain off the excess liquid. Squeeze the spinach by hand to remove as much liquid as possible, then cut it up roughly and put to one side.

Drain and rinse the crab meat to remove the excess salt. Squeeze well to remove as much liq as possible.

Place the breadcrumbs and the grated mozzare in a bowl with the crabmeat and the cooked spinach, bind together with the egg yolk and season to taste with black pepper.

Shape the mixture into eight patties, 7cm (3in) i diameter and 3cm (1¼in) thick.

Heat the oil in a frying pan over a high heat and seal each patty, cooking for 2 minutes on each side until lightly browned. Remove from the pan place on a non-stick baking tray and bake in the oven for 20 minutes until cooked through.

For the sauce, combine the mayonnaise with bo mustards in a small bowl, add the tarragon and season with black pepper to taste.

Serve the baked crab cakes with the mustard ar herb mayonnaise.

COOK'S TIP
A good way to squeeze water out of cooked spinach is to sandwich it between two dinner plates. Press the plates together over the sir until all the water has been extracted.

chicken livers on chargrilled polenta

We love this great combination of smooth chicken livers and crunchy polenta.

30 mins		**539** cals	**22g** fat
prep & cook time	serves 4	per serving	per serving

5 tablespoons olive oil
250g (8oz) block polenta, cut into 8 x 1cm (½in) slices
1 red pepper, deseeded and cut into 10 large pieces
1 green pepper, deseeded and cut into 10 large pieces
250g (8oz) chicken livers, defrosted if frozen
2 cloves garlic, finely chopped
20g (¾oz) fresh sage, finely chopped

Heat 3 tablespoons of oil in a large ridged griddle pan or frying pan until very hot, sear each side of the polenta for 1 minute, then turn the heat down slightly and continue to cook for 5 minutes on each side. Heat the remaining oil in a large frying pan and cook the red and green peppers until softened. Remove them from the pan and keep warm.

Add the chicken livers and cook for 5-7 minutes or until cooked through, adding the garlic and sage one minute before the end. Remove the chicken livers from the pan and arrange with the peppers, garlic and sage on top of the polenta.

COOK'S TIPS
Cook the chicken livers until there is no pink colour in the centre, but be careful not to overcook as they will become tough and leathery.

If you can't find ready-made polenta, buy the quick-cook variety - cook according to packet instructions, leave to cool in a greased tin and slice when cool.

herb-roasted chicken with lemon & caper sauce

A great alternative to the traditional Sunday roast!

:30: mins		692 cals	58g fat
prep & cook time	serves 4	per serving	per serving

00g (3¹/₂oz) unsalted butter, softened.

0g (³/₄oz) flat leaf parsley, chopped

teaspoon freshly chopped tarragon

clove garlic, crushed

boneless chicken breasts, skin on

slices Parma ham

00ml (3¹/₂fl oz) dry white wine

75ml (9fl oz) fresh chicken stock

75ml (9fl oz) double cream, or half-fat crème fraîche

uice of 1 lemon

tablespoons capers

alt and freshly ground black pepper

reheat the oven to 190°C/375°F/gas mark 5.

Mix the butter, half the parsley, the tarragon, garlic and seasoning together. Divide into four and place evenly under the skin of each chicken reast. Wrap 1 slice of Parma ham around each reast.

our the wine and stock into a saucepan, bring the boil and reduce by half. Remove from he heat.

Heat a frying pan and carefully cook the chicken for 1-2 minutes on each side. Transfer the chicken to a baking sheet and cook in the preheated oven for about 20 minutes, until cooked through (the juices will run clear when a skewer is inserted in the centre).

Return the stock to the heat, add the cream and bring to the boil. Remove from the heat and add the lemon juice, capers, remaining parsley and salt and pepper to taste.

Place a chicken breast on each plate, spoon over the sauce, and serve immediately with roasted vegetables of your choice.

Variation
Wrap the chicken breasts with slices of streaky bacon instead.

lemon chicken with lemon & sage risotto

A light and tangy main course that's quick and easy enough for a midweek treat.

prep & cook time	serves 4	per serving	per serving
30 mins		524 cals	10g fat

4 chicken breasts, skin on
juice of 3 lemons and zest of 2
1 tablespoon garlic olive oil
300g (10oz) arborio risotto rice
2 chicken stock cubes made up with 900ml (1½ pints)
   boiling water
20g (³/₄oz) sage, finely chopped
50g (2oz) Parmesan, finely grated

Preheat the oven to 220°C/425°F/gas mark 7.

Place the chicken breasts on a baking tray, sprinkle over the juice of 1 lemon and season. Place in the oven and cook for 25 minutes.

In the meantime make the risotto. In a saucepan heat the garlic olive oil, then add the rice and stir to coat in the oil. Gradually add the stock a little at a time, adding more stock as necessary. Continue until all the stock has been used up. This will take approximately 20 minutes.

Finally stir in the sage, Parmesan, the lemon zest and remaining lemon juice, and stir to incorporate.

Pile the risotto onto individual plates and top each with a chicken breast.

COOK'S TIP
Replace the garlic olive oil with ordinary olive oil and gently fry 1 clove of garlic in it before adding the rice.

pan-fried pork with beans

A great winter warmer. Serve with plenty of bread to soak up the juices.

prep &
cook time

serves 4

per
serving

per
serving

5 tablespoons olive oil
100g (3½oz) shallots, peeled and finely chopped
4 pork loin steaks
3 x 410g (13½oz) cans cannellini beans, drained
1 chicken stock cube, made up with 600ml
    (1 pint) boiling water
20g (¾oz) flat-leaf parsley, finely chopped
20g (¾oz) mint, torn into pieces
1 Italian ciabatta loaf
125g (4oz) herb salad

Heat 2 tablespoons of the olive oil in a large frying pan over a medium heat and fry the shallots gently until softened. Add the pork loin steaks and brown on both sides.

Add the cannellini beans and stock, cover and simmer for 15-20 minutes.

Remove the lid, and add the remaining olive oil, the parsley and mint. Serve with ciabatta and a crisp green salad.

COOK'S TIP
Replace the cannellini beans with a can of kidney beans or mixed beans, if you prefer.

garlic & rosemary lamb

You can prepare the marinade up to a day in advance and leave the lamb to absorb its flavours while you get on with the rest of the meal. The actual cooking time is only 20 minutes.

prep & cook time	serves 4	per serving	per serving
2½ hours		353 cals	30g fat

2 tablespoons olive oil
2 cloves garlic, crushed
2-3 tablespoons freshly chopped rosemary
1 teaspoon English mustard
grated zest and juice of 1 lime
4 lamb shoulder chops
salt and freshly ground black pepper

Blend together the oil, garlic, rosemary, mustard, lime zest and juice, and season to taste.

Arrange the chops in a dish and coat with the marinade. Cover and leave to marinate in the refrigerator for 2 hours, turning occasionally.

Place under a moderate grill and grill for 20 minutes or until cooked according to taste, basting occasionally with the marinade. Chunky chips make an ideal accompaniment.

COOK'S TIP
The longer the better as far as marinating is concerned: you can even put it in the fridge the night before. After 24 hours the meat will have been infused with a fantastic flavour.

Variation
Try this with pork chops instead of lamb.

meatballs in tomato sauce

Serve this old family favourite on a bed of rice, spaghetti or ribbon pasta.

30 mins
prep & cook time

serves 4

494 cals
per serving

28g fat
per serving

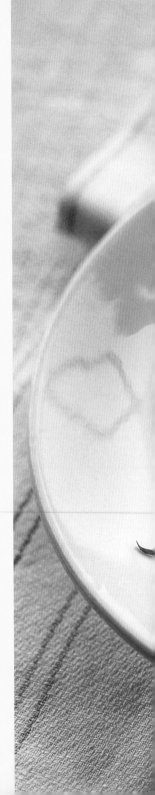

2 slices wholemeal bread, crusts removed
4 tablespoons milk
500g (1lb) extra-lean beef mince
1 tablespoon freshly chopped parsley or chives
4 tablespoons oil
2 onions, chopped
4 x 250g (8oz) cans chopped tomatoes
1 tablespoon tomato purée
handful basil leaves, shredded
250ml (8fl oz) red or white wine or water
salt and freshly ground black pepper

Mash the bread with the milk, then add the mince and parsley or chives. Season and mix well. Divide into 32 portions, and roll each into a little ball.

Heat the oil in a large frying pan and add the meatballs and chopped onion. Brown the meatballs all over.

Add the remaining ingredients, cover and simmer gently for 20 minutes before serving.

pan-fried steak with herby polenta

A great midweek treat. Using quick-cook polenta means you can have dinner on the table in minutes.

30 mins — prep & cook time

serves 4

686 cals — per serving

24g fat — per serving

2 tablespoons olive oil

4 x 125g (4oz) beef sirloin steaks or 500g
(1lb) rump steak cut into 4 equal pieces

2 tablespoons balsamic vinegar

4-6 vine ripened tomatoes, quartered

2 vegetable stock cubes, made up with
2 litres (3½ pints) boiling water

250g (8oz) 1-minute-cook polenta

75g (3oz) flat-leaf parsley, finely chopped

125g (4oz) Parmesan, freshly grated

25g (1oz) butter

125g (4oz) herb salad

First cook the steak. Heat the oil in a frying pan, add the steaks and cook over a moderate heat for 2½ minutes each side for rare, 4 minutes each side for medium and 6 minutes each side for well-done. Remove and keep warm.

Add the balsamic vinegar to the frying pan along with the tomatoes and cook for 2-3 minutes. Put to one side.

Now cook the polenta. Put the stock in a saucepan and bring to the boil over a moderate heat. Add the polenta in a steady stream, stirring continuously. Reduce the heat and cook for 1 minute. Remove from the heat and add the parsley, Parmesan and butter.

Divide the wet polenta between 4 plates, then top with the herb salad and tomatoes, followed by a steak. Serve immediately.

COOK'S TIP
Replace the quick-cook polenta with the ordinary variety - it will take about 15 minutes to cook and require more stirring.

griddled sirloin steak with gorgonzola

A simple but indulgent main course - perfect food for a celebration.

30 mins		356 cals	21g fat
prep & cook time	serves 4	per serving	per serving

4 x 175g (6oz) sirloin steaks, 2.5cm (1in) thick
125g (4oz) Gorgonzola
1 tablespoon oil
125g (4oz) Italian salad leaves
2 tablespoons vinaigrette or salad dressing
1 tablespoon Parmesan, finely grated
salt and freshly ground black pepper

Preheat a heavy-based ridged frying or griddle pan.

Make a horizontal slit in each steak, taking care not to cut completely through, making a pocket to hold the filling. Place a quarter of the Gorgonzola in each pocket. Seal the open edges with a cocktail stick, to prevent the filling from escaping. Season on both sides.

Heat the oil in the frying pan. Cook the steaks over a moderate heat for 2¹⁄₂ minutes each side for rare, 4 minutes each side for medium, and 6-7 minutes each side for well done. Remove and discard the cocktail sticks. Divide the salad between four plates. Drizzle with salad dressing and scatter with Parmesan. Top each plate with a steak and serve immediately.

This recipe works just as well with other Italian cheeses such as taleggio, freshly sliced Parmesan, Provolone and Assiego.

COOK'S TIP
For basic vinaigrette, whisk together 6 tablespoons oil, 2 tablespoons vinegar and 1 teaspoon mustard. Season, and use straightaway or keep in a jar in the fridge for up to a week.

vegetable dishes

mozzarella & tomato salad

A delicious starter or light lunch, this combination of ripe tomatoes and buffalo mozzarella will carry you straight back to Italy.

20 mins		**234** cals	**21**g fat
prep & cook time	serves 4	per serving	per serving

150g (5oz) buffalo mozzarella, thinly sliced
3 ripe tomatoes, sliced
50g (2oz) black olives
3 tablespoons virgin olive oil
3 teaspoons white wine vinegar
1 teaspoon coarse-grain mustard
2 tablespoons chopped fresh oregano or basil
freshly ground black pepper

Arrange the cheese, tomatoes and olives on a serving dish.

Combine the remaining ingredients in a screw top jar and shake well.

Pour the dressing over the salad and serve immediately.

COOK'S TIP
For a more substantial lunch, add a sliced avocado and serve with crusty bread.

broad bean purée

Broad beans have a beautiful colour and texture that is much under-rated – give this purée a go and prepare to be converted!

| prep & cook time | serves 4-6 | per serving | per serving |

250g (8oz) potatoes, cut into small pieces
250g (8oz) shelled broad beans, thawed if frozen
4-5 tablespoons olive oil
1 garlic clove, crushed
75g (3oz) pecorino or Parmesan, grated
salt and freshly ground black pepper

Preheat the oven to 220°C/425°F/gas mark 7.

Cook the potatoes in boiling salted water for 5-10 minutes or until tender, then drain. Cook the beans separately in boiling salted water for 5 minutes or until tender, then drain and cool. Remove the skins if necessary

Put the beans and potatoes in a bowl, add the oil, garlic and three-quarters of the cheese, and mash well together.

Season with salt and pepper, stir well and spoon into four ramekins.

Sprinkle with the remaining cheese and bake in the oven for 10-15 minutes or until the cheese is browned and bubbling. Serve immediately.

Serve alongside grilled meat or fish as a vegetable side dish, or as a starter with stri of toast.

COOK'S TIP
Frozen broad beans are often ready-skinned. using fresh broad beans, cook for 5 minutes boiling salted water, leave to cool slightly, then slip the brilliant green beans out of the outer greyish skins. It takes a while but it's worth it in terms of both colour and texture.

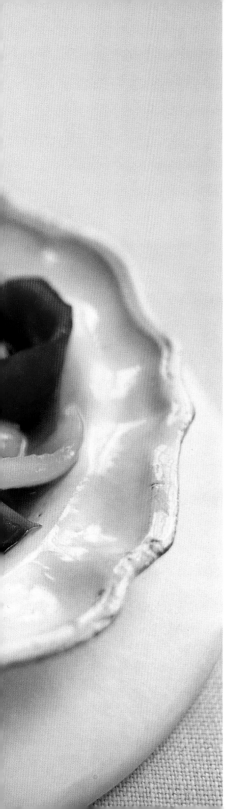

peperonata

These sweet-and-sour peppers are the perfect accompaniment to fresh pasta or grilled meat, or you can just pile them up on crusty bread for a quick lunch.

30 mins	**¶¶**	**235** cals	**17**g fat
prep & cook time	serves 4	per serving	per serving

2 red peppers
2 green peppers
2 orange or yellow peppers
6 tablespoons olive oil
4 tablespoons red wine vinegar
25g (1oz) caster sugar
salt

Deseed and slice the peppers into long strips.

Heat the oil in a heavy-based saucepan and add the peppers, tossing well to coat them in the oil.

Fry over a low heat, covered, for 30 minutes, until the peppers are soft.

Remove the pan from the heat and stir in the vinegar, sugar and salt to taste.

COOK'S TIP
Don't be tempted to make this dish with green peppers only – the red and orange or yellow peppers add a touch of sweetness that makes all the difference.

balsamic roasted shallots & parmesan shavings with parma ham

Transform a humble vegetable into a stylish accompaniment! Replace the Parma ham with toasted pine kernels for a tasty meat-free alternative.

| prep & cook time | serves 4 | per serving | per serving |

1 tablespoon olive oil
300g (10oz) shallots, peeled
1 teaspoon brown sugar
1 teaspoon fresh thyme leaves
250ml (8fl oz) balsamic dressing
75g (3oz) Parma ham
25g (1oz) Parmesan shavings

COOK'S TIP
To make a balsamic vinaigrette, whisk together 6 tablespoons oil, 2 tablespoons balsamic vinegar and 1 teaspoon of mustard. Season to taste and use straight away or keep in a jar in the fridge for up to a week.

In a large frying pan heat the olive oil and fry the shallots gently for 5 minutes.

Next add the brown sugar, thyme and dressing. Cover the pan and simmer gently for 25-30 minutes or until the liquid has reduced and the shallots are soft. Cool.

To serve, pile the shallots onto individual serving plates, top with the ham and finish with the Parmesan cheese shavings. Serve immediately.

carrot batons with prosciutto

Tender sweet carrots and salty ham make a great combination. Throw in a few toasted pine kernels for extra crunch.

25 mins	serves 4	152 cals	10g fat
prep & cook time	serves 4	per serving	per serving

2 tablespoons olive oil
1 small onion, finely chopped
4 slices prosciutto ham, finely chopped
350g (11½oz) carrot batons
100ml (3½fl oz) chicken stock
1 tablespoon fresh parsley, finely chopped
a drizzle virgin olive oil
salt and freshly ground black pepper

Heat the oil in a saucepan over a moderate heat and fry the onion gently for 2-3 minutes. Add the prosciutto and cook for a further minute, then add the carrots and chicken stock and season to taste.

Cover and cook gently for 5-10 minutes until the carrots are tender. Toss the parsley through the carrots and serve in a warm bowl with a drizzle of olive oil.

Variation
Replace the prosciutto with a handful of toasted pine kernels for a vegetarian alternative.

basil-scented braised fennel

Braising fennel until it is meltingly tender transforms its aniseed flavour into a mild and mellow sweetness.

30 mins		164 cals	16g fat
prep & cook time	serves 4	per serving	per serving

4 tablespoons olive oil
3 large fennel bulbs, trimmed and cut into
1cm (1/2in) thick wedges – reserve the
green fronds
1 vegetable stock cube, made up with 150ml
(1/4 pint) boiling water
handful shredded basil leaves
salt and freshly ground black pepper

Heat the oil in a large flameproof casserole dish.

Add the fennel wedges and cook for 5-8 minutes until golden brown, turning carefully with the aid of a fork.

Pour in the stock, cover, and simmer gently for 20 minutes until the fennel is tender. Add the basil and seasoning 1 minute before the end of the cooking time.

Serve with griddled meat or fish and the reduced cooking liquor. Decorate with the reserved fennel fronds.

fruity baked aubergines & peppers

A versatile dish that can be served as an accompaniment to meat or fish, or added to pasta to make a tasty vegetarian main course.

| prep & cook time | serves 4-6 | per serving | per serving |

125ml (4fl oz) olive oil

2 medium aubergines, sliced lengthways into 1cm (1/2in) thick slices

2 red peppers, deseeded and cut into quarters

20g (3/4oz) thyme, leaves removed from the stems

25g (1oz) pine kernels

25g (1oz) sultanas

salt and freshly ground black pepper

Variations

Cook wedges of red onion with the aubergines and peppers for a touch of added sweetness.

Toss the vegetables with cooked pasta and add cubes of mozzarella or feta cheese for a delicious vegetarian supper.

Preheat the oven to 200°C/400°F/gas mark 6.

Using a tablespoon of the olive oil, lightly oil a large baking sheet, then place the aubergines and peppers on the tray in a single layer.

Brush liberally with the remaining olive oil, then sprinkle with thyme and season with salt and freshly ground black pepper.

Bake in the oven for 15-20 minutes, adding the pine kernels and sultanas a couple of minutes before the cooking time is complete. Serve immediately.

warm chickpeas with red chard & asparagus

A fantastic combination of flavours and textures – make sure you have some crusty bread to mop up the delicious tomato-y juices!

| prep & cook time | serves 6 | per serving | per serving |

2 tablespoons olive oil
1 red onion, peeled and finely chopped
1 red chilli, deseeded and finely chopped
250ml (8fl oz) white wine
1 tablespoon tomato purée
200g (7oz) red Swiss chard, washed and finely shredded, or Swiss chard
2 x 410g (13½oz) tins chickpeas, drained
125g (4oz) fine asparagus tips, cut in half, blanched and refreshed
20g (³/₄oz) fresh flat-leaf parsley, leaves removed from the stem

In a large frying pan or wok heat the oil then fry the onion and chilli gently for 2-3 minutes until softened. Add the wine and tomato purée and cook until reduced by half.

Add the red chard, chickpeas and asparagus and cook for a further 2-3 minutes. Transfer to a serving bowl and sprinkle with the parsley leaves. Serve immediately.

Variation
Use tinned borlotti beans instead of chickpeas.

tomatoes stuffed with mascarpone, spinach & gorgonzola

Stuffed tomatoes have never been so stylish!

prep & cook time   serves 4   279 cals per serving   24g fat per serving

4 large beef steak tomatoes, or 8 large
   plum tomatoes
50g (2oz) unsalted butter
500g (1lb) spinach
4 tablespoons mascarpone
½ teaspoon freshly grated nutmeg
75g (3oz) Gorgonzola, crumbled
salt and freshly ground black pepper

Use grated Cheddar instead of Gorgonzola if you don't like blue cheese.

This dish will be even quicker to prepare if you use frozen spinach instead of fresh. Defrost before using and drain off any liquid that results before adding to the pan.

Mascarpone is a thick cream cheese quite similar to crème fraîche.

Preheat the oven to 190°C/375°F/gas mark 5.

Slice the tops off the tomatoes and gently scoop out the seeds using a teaspoon.

Heat the butter in a large frying pan, add the spinach and let it wilt, gently stirring for 2-3 minutes. Stir in the mascarpone. Season with a little nutmeg, salt and freshly ground black pepper.

Carefully fill the tomatoes. Place in an ovenproof dish and sprinkle over the Gorgonzola.

Bake in the preheated oven for 15-20 minutes or until the cheese is browned. Serve immediately.

tuscan potato salad

We love this simple light salad. Perfect for summer lunches, picnics or barbecues.

prep & cook time	serves 4-6	per serving	per serving
30 mins		185 cals	5g fat

1kg (2lb) Charlotte or Anya salad potatoes, cut in half if large
150ml (¼ pint) low-fat natural yogurt
2 tablespoons lemon juice
6 salad onions, finely sliced
10 black pitted olives, cut in half
8 anchovy fillets, snipped into 1cm (½in) pieces, optional
1 tablespoon flat-leaf parsley, chopped finely

Place the potatoes in a saucepan, cover with cold water and lightly salt. Bring to the boil, then cover and simmer for 20 minutes or until tender.

When the potatoes are cool, drain and gently stir in the remaining ingredients. Chill until required.

desserts

watermelon granita

Nothing could be simpler than this refreshing water ice – the perfect end to a summer meal.

4¹/₂ hrs		**170** cals	**0**g fat
prep time	serves 4	per serving	per serving

625g (1¹/₄lb) watermelon (rindless weight)
125g (4oz) caster sugar
600ml (1 pint) water
3 tablespoons lemon juice
sprigs of mint and slices of melon, to decorate

Place the watermelon in a food processor or liquidiser and blend to a smooth purée. Add the sugar, water and lemon juice, and process again.

Press the mixture through a fine nylon sieve to remove the seeds. Pour into a suitable freezer container, cover with a lid and place in the freezer for 2 hours.

Remove and stir so that the ice that has formed around the sides and base of the container is mixed into the unfrozen centre, then re-cover and return to the freezer for another hour.

Remove, mix thoroughly again and then re-freeze for a further hour.

Although you need to allow four hours' total freezing time, the actual time you need to spend in preparing this dessert is minimal.

COOK'S TIP
If you have an ice-cream maker, this granita will be even easier to make. Just follow the manufacturer's instructions.

bruléed fruit with amaretto & mascarpone

Creamy mascarpone and a dash of alcohol lend a touch of luxury to this fruity dessert.

30 mins		296 cals	17g fat
prep & cook time	serves 6	per serving	per serving

125g (4oz) dark brown soft sugar
2-3 tablespoons Amaretto or fruit liqueur
4 peaches or nectarines, stoned and cut
  into wedges
3 fresh, ripe figs, quartered
250g (8oz) mascarpone

Place half the sugar and the Amaretto in a saucepan over a moderate heat and stir until the sugar has dissolved.

Add the peaches or nectarines and cook for 2-3 minutes, stirring occasionally. Remove from the heat, stir in the figs and transfer the fruit and juices to a heatproof serving dish. Allow to cool.

Spread the mascarpone over the fruit and sprinkle over the remaining sugar.

Place under a preheated hot grill for 2-3 minutes until the sugar has melted and caramelised. Delicious served hot or cold.

COOK'S TIP
Replace the fruit with whatever is in season - try plums instead of peaches later in the year.

99

panna cotta with sparkling peaches

A classic Italian treat – prepare well in advance for indulgence on demand!

4¹/₂ hrs | **serves 8** | **419 cals** | **38g fat**
prep time | serves 8 | per serving | per serving

586ml (1 pint) double cream
1 vanilla pod, seeds removed and reserved
zest of 1 lemon, peeled off in long strips
40g (1¹/₂oz) unrefined golden caster sugar
2 teaspoons powdered gelatine
2 tablespoons cold water
2 peaches
400ml (14fl oz) sparkling white wine

Pour the cream into a small saucepan, add the vanilla seeds, lemon zest and sugar, then heat gently until the sugar dissolves.

Place the gelatine and water in a cup or ramekin, stand in a saucepan with a small amount of boiling water in it and allow the gelatine to dissolve. (Do not let the gelatine get too hot.)

Take the cream off the heat, remove the lemon zest and whisk in the gelatine until it dissolves. Pour into individual cups or ramekins. Refrigerate for at least four hours, or overnight, until set.

Remove the stones from the peaches and slice. Pour over the sparkling wine, cover and put to one side until required. Just before serving the dessert, pour off the wine, place it in a small saucepan and reduce it down until only 100ml (3¹/₂fl oz) of syrupy liquid remains.

To serve, decorate each cup or ramekin with the fresh peaches and pour a few spoonfuls of syrup over the top of each.

Allow at least four hours' setting time for this dessert. It can be prepared up to 24 hours in advance and stored in the fridge.

For an alternative presentation, place the base of each cup or ramekin in warm water to loosen the panna cotta and then turn out onto a serving plate. Spoon over the peaches and syrup and serve.

strawberry pannetone with fromage frais & honey

Use plump juicy strawberries in season, or bananas in winter, for this simple, satisfying dessert.

25 mins	serves 6	420 cals	19g fat
prep & cook time	serves 6	per serving	per serving

6 slices of pannetone or brioche
300g (10oz) strawberries or 3 bananas, thinly sliced
zest and juice of 1 orange or lemon
200ml (7fl oz) fromage frais
2 tablespoons honey

Preheat the grill to a medium heat and lay the sliced pannetone on top of the grill pan. In a large bowl, mix the fruit with the orange or lemon zest and juice and combine gently. Arrange the fruit over the surface of the bread.

Place under the grill and cook until golden and hot - approximately 5-6 minutes.

To serve, slide onto plates, put a generous spoonful of fromage frais in the middle of each, drizzle over the honey and serve immediately.

Panettone is a large, sweet, fruity bread with a domed top which is often used in Italian desserts.

tiramisù

This classic and wicked dessert looks stunning in simple glass dishes.

prep time	serves 6	per serving	per serving
2½ hrs		679 cals	51g fat

175ml (6fl oz) strong black coffee
3 tablespoons Marsala or sherry
3 tablespoons brandy
8 trifle sponges
250g (8oz) tub mascarpone
300ml (½ pint) double cream, lightly whipped
4 level tablespoons icing sugar, sifted
25g (1oz) cocoa powder

Mix together the coffee, Marsala and brandy. Place 4 trifle sponges in a serving dish and pour over half the coffee mixture.

Mix together the mascarpone, cream and icing sugar and spoon half over the sponges.

Place the remaining trifle sponges on top, and pour over the remaining coffee mixture.

Top with the rest of the mascarpone mixture and smooth the surface. Sieve cocoa over the top and chill for at least 2-3 hours before serving.

Allow 2 hours' chilling time for this dessert. The actual preparation doesn't take long at all.

Variation
Replace the double cream with half-fat crème fraîche for a lower-fat alternative.

cassata

A real family favourite, this is the perfect treat on a hot summer's day.

30 mins		387 cals	17g fat
prep & cook time	serves 4	per serving	per serving

300g (10oz) vanilla ice cream
75g (3oz) amaretti biscuits
100g (3½oz) luxury mixed dried fruit
25g (1oz) toasted flaked almonds
50g (2oz) plain chocolate

Remove the ice cream from its container and transfer to a mixing bowl. Allow to soften slightly. Crumble the biscuits into the ice cream and add the dried fruit and the almonds. Gently mix to incorporate all the ingredients.

Pile into a small freezerproof bowl or ice cream container and place in the coldest part of the freezer for at least 20 minutes.

Melt the chocolate in a heatproof bowl over a pan of gently simmering water. Remove from the heat.

When ready to serve, scoop the ice cream onto chilled serving plates and drizzle with the melted chocolate. Serve immediately.

lemon, almond and pear cake

We couldn't resist this traditional Italian fruit cake - make it in advance and store in a tin for an instant pudding every day of the week.

| prep & cook time | serves 12 | per serving | per serving |

250g (8oz) unsalted butter, softened
250g (8oz) caster sugar
4 large eggs
50g (2oz) plain flour
250g (8oz) ground almonds
½ teaspoon almond essence
grated zest and juice of 2 lemons
4 ripe pears, peeled, halved and fanned out
4 tablespoons apricot jam, warmed and
  sieved

Preheat the oven to 180°C/350°F/gas mark 4.

Line the base of a 20cm (8in) springform cake tin with parchment paper.

In a bowl cream together the butter and sugar until soft and creamy. Beat in the eggs one at a time adding some flour after each addition.

When all the eggs and flour have been incorporated fold in the almonds, almond essence, lemon zest and juice.

Spoon the cake mixture into the prepared tin and smooth the surface with the back of a spoon. Top with the fanned out pears. Place in the preheated oven and bake for 1 hour or until a skewer inserted into the centre of the cake comes out clean. If the cake seems to be browning too quickly, cover with a piece of foil.

Glaze with the apricot jam while still warm and allow the cake to cool before removing from the tin.

basics

tomato sauce

Delicious and infinitely adaptable.

prep & cook time   serves 4   163 cals per serving   15g fat per serving

4 tablespoons olive oil
2 cloves garlic, chopped
500g (1lb) ripe tomatoes, skinned and
chopped coarsely, or 400g (13oz) can chopped
    tomatoes
1 tablespoon finely chopped fresh oregano
1 teaspoon sugar
salt and freshly ground black pepper

Heat the oil in a saucepan and gently fry the
garlic for 2 minutes.

Add the remaining ingredients and cook over a
moderately high heat for 25-30 minutes,
uncovered, until thickened, stirring frequently.

To make a quick Bolognese Sauce:
Fry 500g (1lb) lean beef mince and 2 chopped
onions in the oil for 10-15 minutes until the
mince is browned. Add the garlic and continue as
above. For a thicker Bolognese sauce, add 1
tablespoon of cornflour blended with 2
tablespoons water to the pan at the same time
as the tomatoes.

Variation
Replace the fresh oregano with dried basil, or a
mixture of dried basil and dried oregano.

**Both tomato sauce and Bolognese sauce
freeze well - make a big batch and freeze it in
individual portions for convenience.**

pasta carbonara

Another classic sauce.

prep & cook time   serves 4   634 cals per serving   29g fat per serving

375g (12oz) long pasta such as spaghetti or
    tagliatelle
175g (6oz) pancetta cubetti, or streaky bacon,
    cut into small pieces
1 egg
4 tablespoons single cream
40g (1½oz) Parmesan cheese, grated
salt and freshly ground pepper

Cook the pasta following pack instructions in a
large saucepan of boiling water.

Fry the pancetta or bacon in a large frying pan
over a moderate heat until crisp and golden.
Remove from the pan and drain on kitchen
paper.

In a small mixing bowl, best the egg with the
cream and the Parmesan and season to taste.

When the pasta is cooked, drain well and return
to the pan, over a low heat. Add the egg mixture
and the bacon and stir over a low heat until the
mixture has thickened slightly. Be careful not to
overcook, or you will end up with scrambled egg.

Serve immediately.

pesto genovese

Fresh pesto is simple to make and it bursts with flavour. Pesto can be kept for up to a week in the refrigerator, and it freezes well too. It's traditionally made with basil, but we think our variations are delicious too.

prep time	serves 4	per serving	per serving

20 large basil leaves
6 cloves garlic, peeled and crushed
50g (2oz) pine kernels
125g (4oz) Parmesan cheese, grated
250ml (8fl oz) olive oil
salt and freshly ground black pepper

Purée the basil, garlic, pine kernels and cheese in a blender or food processor. If using a blender add a little of the olive oil before you start blending. With the motor running, pour in the olive oil in a slow steady stream so that the sauce emulsifies. Taste for seasoning.

Variations
Coriander and Parsley Pesto Whizz up an onion and a large handful of coriander and parsley in the food processor. Drizzle in two tablespoons of red wine vinegar and 175ml (6fl oz) olive oil until mixed. Transfer to a serving bowl and stir in 40g (1½oz) cashew nuts. Serve.

Rocket Pesto Combine 100g (3½oz) rocket, 50g (2oz) pine kernels, 2 cloves garlic, 50g (2oz) Parmesan cheese and 15g (½oz) pecorino cheese in a food processor and mix until creamy. Gradually add 6 tablespoons olive oil and mix until combined.

Walnut Pesto Place 75g (3oz) walnuts, 75g (3oz) Parmesan or pecorino cheese, 2 cloves garlic and 15g (½oz) parsley in a food processor and blend until the ingredients are roughly chopped. Add the oil slowly and blend again.

pizza bases

A simple bread dough is the recipe for a successful pizza base. See page 48 for some great topping ideas.

prep & cook time **serves 4** **per serving** **per serving**

250g (9oz) strong white bread flour
¼ teaspoon salt
6g (¹⁄₄oz) sachet easy blend dried yeast
1 tablespoon olive oil
approximately 150ml (¼ pint) warm water

Put the flour, salt and yeast in a large bowl and mix well. Using a wooden spoon, stir in the oil and enough warm water to make a soft but manageable dough. (Alternatively, put the flour, salt and yeast in a food processor. Add the liquid and blend for 2--3 minutes.)

Knead the dough on a floured surface for 10 minutes or until smooth and elastic. Grease a large polythene bag with a drop of olive oil, put the dough inside and leave it to rise in a warm place for about 30 minutes or until doubled in size.

Turn the dough out to a work surface and knead it for 3-5 minutes, then return it to the polythene bag and leave it to rise for a further 30 minutes.

Turn the dough out onto a work surface again, knock it back and knead briefly.

Preheat the oven to 220°C/425°F/gas mark 7.

If you prefer a base of about 1cm (¹⁄₂in) thick, roll out a circle of dough 30cm (10in) diameter. Grease a large baking tray and place the base on top. Top the base with a tomato sauce, cheese and any toppings you like. Cook in the centre of the oven for approximately 18-20 minutes or until crisp and golden.

For a thinner base, roll out the dough into 2 circles, 30cm (12in) in diameter and treat as above. Reduce the cooking time to approximately 12-14 minutes.

ciabatta

If you fancy the 'home-baked' taste, try this traditional bread recipe. Once made, you can use it to make bruschetta and crostini (pages 22 and 24), or just eat it as it is!

8 hours	makes 4 loaves	740 cals	16g fat
prep & cook time		per loaf	per loaf

Starter dough
375g (12oz) plain flour
/₄ teaspoon easy blend yeast
200ml (7fl oz) water at room temperature

300ml (½ pint) warm water
5 tablespoons milk, warmed slightly
1 tablespoon olive oil

625g (1¼lb) plain flour
1 teaspoon easy blend yeast
1 tablespoon salt

Flour to dust

Sift the flour and the yeast together in a large mixing bowl and slowly mix in the water. Mix thoroughly for five minutes until the dough is soft and sticky. Cover the bowl with cling film and leave to rise in a warm place for 3-4 hours until it has tripled in size and looks bubbly and foamy. Chill until ready to use. It will keep in this state for up to 3 days.

Remove the starter dough from the fridge an hour before making the ciabatta. Stir the warm water, milk and olive oil into the starter mixture.

Slowly add this mixture to the flour, adding the yeast and salt.

Using either a food processor with a dough hook, or your hands, knead the dough on a floured surface until smooth and springy, but still slightly sticky. Put the dough into an oiled bowl, cover and leave to rise until doubled in size.

Using floured hands, divide the sticky dough into four and stretch into rectangles, pulling it out and pressing it flat. You may have to use a spatula to help. Cover with a damp cloth and leave in a warm place for 2 hours.

Preheat the oven to 220°C/425°F/gas mark 7. Place baking sheets in the oven to heat.

When the ciabatta is ready to cook, sprinkle the heated baking sheets with flour and place the dough on top, using a spatula for support if necessary.

Spray the inside of the oven with water before placing the loaves inside to bake for 20-25 minutes, spraying with water three more times during the first 10 minutes.

Remove from the oven when golden and crusty. Transfer to a cooling rack and allow to cool for 45 minutes before slicing and serving.

pasta dough

Freshly made pasta topped with your favourite sauce is just perfect. This is the basic recipe, which you can then adapt.

prep & cook time | serves 8 | per serving | per serving

425g (14oz) pasta flour
½ teaspoon salt
4 medium eggs

Sift the flour and the salt into a large bowl, make a well in the middle and crack the eggs into the well. Mix the eggs into the flour and knead into a ball. Remove from the bowl and knead the dough on a lightly floured surface for 15 minutes until smooth.

Shape into a ball, return to the bowl and cover with a clean, damp cloth. Rest for at least 30 minutes.

The dough is now ready to make into your preferred pasta shape. If you have a pasta machine, follow the manufacturer's instructions.

If you don't have a pasta machine, there are several alternatives:

To make tortellini, roll the pasta dough out thinly and cut out circles 5cm (2in) in diameter. Put a little of your chosen filling in the middle of each circle, and fold over to a half-moon shape. Wind each one around your finger like a ring and press the ends together. Cook in boiling salted water for 2–3 minutes until al dente.

To make ravioli, divide the pasta into two portions. Roll each portion out thinly into large rectangles. Lay out one large pasta sheet on a work surface and dot with half-teaspoonfuls of your chosen mixture in regular rows. Brush the rows in between the mounds of mixture with water, lay the second sheet over the top and press down in between the rows. Use a pasta cutter or a knife to cut down the rows. Cook in boiling salted water for 4–5 minutes until al dente.

To make lasagne, roll the dough out very thinly and cut into squares or rectangles of the required. Use in the recipe on page 44.

To make tagliatelle, roll the dough out very thinly and cut into strips. Hang the strips over the handles of wooden spoons or on a clean wooden chair back to dry. Cook in boiling salted water for 1–2 minutes until al dente.

Variations
To make pasta verde
Add 150g (5oz) cooked spinach to the flour. You may not need all the eggs.

To make tomato pasta
Add 2 tablespoons tomato purée to the pasta dough.

potato gnocchi

An Italian classic that is as delicious as it is simple to prepare.

30 mins		179 cals	1g fat
prep time	serves 4-6	per serving	per serving

500g (1lb) potatoes, peeled and cut into chunks
100g (3^1/$_2$oz) plain or wholemeal flour
^{1}/$_2$-1 teaspoon salt

Boil the potatoes in salted water for 15-20 minutes or until tender. Drain and mash the potatoes until smooth, then add the flour and salt and draw the mixture together. Turn out onto a lightly floured surface and knead until the dough is smooth and uniform.

Divide the dough into four pieces and shape each piece, using plenty of flour, into a long roll about 2cm (3/4in) thick. Cut the rolls across into equal-size rounds (they will flatten slightly as you cut, but this does not matter).

For an attractive ridged effect, place your thumb in the back of each gnocchi and press the tines of a fork lightly on the other side.

Bring a large saucepan of salted water to the boil and add the gnocchi. Cook for 3-5 minutes or until the gnocchi rise to the surface and the water starts to boil again, then remove them with a slotted spoon.

Gnocchi can be made and served straightaway with a sauce of your choice. Or you can make them in advance, turn into a baking dish, add sauce and a sprinkling of cheese and bake when you are ready to eat.

index